THE TRIANGLE CONCEPT, "THE ROAD TO A NEW LIFE"

RANDALL A. VENSON

The Triangle of Life Institute

The Triangle Concept: The Road to a New Life
Randall A. Venson

Published by The Triangle of Life Institute

Copyright © 2023 by Randall A. Venson

ISBN: 979-8-218-25858-0

Printed in the United States of America—First Printing

DEDICATION

This is dedicated to everyone who helped to shape my thinking.

–Randall A. Venson

Acknowledgements

I give all thanks and praise to the creator of the heavens and the earth.

I bear witness God is the creator of all that are living and not living.

I bear witness that God is all-knowing, all forgiving, all loving, all compassionate, and all other positive attributes.

Before God there was none and after God there will be no more. All praises to the creator for the good of the world.

To my family and friends, I love you.

To my son, always seek knowledge, never be a follower, think for yourself, be compassionate with wisdom, and want for your fellow human beings what you would want for yourself.

Always remember to control yourself or someone will control you.

~Randall A. Venson

This is dedicated to all the people who helped shape my thinking.

Table of Contents

► INTRODUCTION ◄

Declaration of War on Ignorance

I am declaring war on ignorance. Ignorance is defined as the lack of knowledge, information, or education. This book would not be possible were it not for ignorance. Ignorance is far and away the biggest threat to the survival of humanity. No problem can be solved, no addiction can be overcome, no democracy can be maintained, and no freedom can be secured as long as ignorance prevails.

Ignorance has killed more people and has been a bigger expense than all the wars combined— because every war has its roots in ignorance. Many people attribute wars to power, greed, and the conquest for territory. While it is true that these are strong motivations that start wars, it is the ignorance of people who enable them to be carried out. It is ignorance that has made slavery possible throughout the world.

I firmly believe that overcoming ignorance is the key to overcoming drug abuse, alcoholism, marginalization, self-hatred, and poverty.

If ignorance is the sickness, then knowledge is the cure.

"Emancipate yourself from mental slavery,
none but ourselves can free our mind."

-- Bob Marley
Redemption Song

► PREFACE ◄

WHY THE ROAD TO EMANCIPATION?

On April 3, 1968, Martin Luther King gave his final speech. In the speech called, "I've Been to the Mountaintop," Rev. King stated, *"We've got some difficult days ahead. But it really doesn't matter to me now, because I've been to the mountaintop. And I don't mind. Like anybody, I would like to live - a long life; longevity has its place. But I am not concerned about that now. I just want to do God's will. And He's allowed me to go up to the mountain. And I've looked over, and I've seen the Promised Land."*

Today, in July of 2015, we have some difficult days in America. The spirits of many of our citizens have been broken by disappointment, hurt, and neglect. A study by Harvard and the National Institute of Mental Health claims that 46% of all Americans will at some point develop a mental disorder.

In 2008 an estimated 20.1 million Americans aged 12 or older were found to be illicit drug users. This is based on results from the 2008 National Survey in Drug Use and Health conducted by the Substance Abuse and Mental Health Services Administration of the U.S. Department of Health and Human services.

There are 17.6 million American adults who abuse alcohol or are alcohol dependent. This according to the 2001-2002 Nation Epidemiological Survey on alcohol-related conditions conducted by the U.S. National Institute on Alcohol Abuse and Alcoholism.

There are so many people who are risking having a healthy triangle. On a single night in America on January 2013, 610,042 were experiencing homelessness. U.S. Census reported that 1,872,020 people in the U.S. were living in poverty. According to the Brain Research Institute, the total number of high school dropouts annually is 3,030,000. 8300 drop out daily.

The Bureau Justice Statistics (BJS) states there are 1,610,446 men and women in prison. The number of drug offenders in prison is 265,800 or 20% in all state prisons. Of the people that are incarcerated in BJS in America 93% are Black men, age 20-39. Twenty-five percent of the world's incarcerated people live in America, although we total only five percent of the world's population.

"There are difficult days ahead," Dr. Martin Luther King quoted in his last speech. He could have no idea just how difficult they would be. As grim as these statistics may sound, I choose to remain optimistic. In the work of a song sung by the Funkadelics "Free Your Mind and Your Behind Will Follow. The road to emancipation leads you to a "free mind."

"Freedom without knowledge is an illusion."
-- Randall Venson, 1999 Independent Presidential Run

1 THE GAME OF LIFE CONCEPT

Before we are even born, we are dealt a set of cards that we have no control over.

I call it NCO — No Control Over

✦ We have no control over who our parents are.

✦ We have no control over our economic condition.

✦ We have no control over the community in which we live.

✦ We have no control over the family we inherit.

We have no control over our race or ethnicity.

The cards we are dealt will be the hand we have to play in this game that we call life.

 # Notes

_____

_____

_____

_____

_____

_____

_____

_____

_____

_____

2 WHO ARE YOU?

- The Cards Dealt

- What's Your Condition?/Personal Resume

- Emotional Report Card

- Character Assessment

- Personal Character Report Card

 # Notes

_____

_____

_____

_____

_____

_____

_____

_____

_____

►The Cards Dealt◄

The cards that James has been dealt in life put him at an enormous disadvantage to John.

The odds are high that James will be sent to prison. While, someone with the cards John has been dealt will be the prosecutor that sends him there.

How does James overcome such a hand?

James must take advantage of any opportunities he is fortunate enough to receive.

<table>
<tr><td>

James

- Single-parent household

- Poor community with a high crime rate

- Poor schools/ limited resources

- Poor role-models

- Poverty stricken

</td><td>

John

- Educated professionally by employed parents

- Solidly affluent community

- Good schools with resources

- Successful role models

- Affluent

</td></tr>
</table>

 # Notes

_____

_____

_____

_____

_____

_____

_____

_____

_____

_____

► What cards were you dealt at birth? ◄

Remember:
You had no control over those cards dealt!

The cards that you are dealt in your life are what I call the lifeline triangle, which I will explain in Chapter 3.

The cards you are dealt at birth will shape the foundation of who you will become. The effects will be either negative or positive depending on how you play your cards.

Family	Community	Who you are
• Single or both parents	• Poor	• Race
• Loving parents	• Middle class	• Religion
• Loving family	• Wealthy	• Gender
• Family with secure structure		• Ethnicity
• Family with insecure structure		• Sex

The cards that you are dealt in your life are what I call the lifeline triangle, which I will explain in Chapter 3.

The cards you are dealt at birth will shape the foundation of who you will become. The effects will be either negative or positive depending on how you play your cards.

 # Notes

_____

_____

_____

_____

_____

_____

_____

_____

_____

_____

What's Your Condition?

Personal Resume	
Name	
Parents/Family	
Employment	
Education	
Skills	
Substance Abuse/ Addiction	
Married/ Single	
Housing Situation	

 # Notes

_____

_____

_____

_____

_____

_____

_____

_____

_____

_____

Your Emotional Report Card is your personal assessment of your emotions.

Emotional Report Card

Condition	Yes	No
Anger		
Fears		
Hurts		
Self-hatred		
Suicidal		

If you answered yes to any of the above, please explain why.

Anger:

Fears:

Hurts:

Self-Hatred:

Suicidal:

 # Notes

_____

_____

_____

_____

_____

_____

_____

_____

_____

_____

Character Assessment
List your character weaknesses

1. _____

2. _____

3. _____

4. _____

5. _____

Have you harmed others close to you?_____

Have you sought forgiveness?_____

 # Notes

_____

_____

_____

_____

_____

_____

_____

_____

_____

Personal Character Report Card

Characteristics	High	Aver-age	Low	Not At All
Self-Esteem				
Kindness				
Cruel				
Compassionate				
Positive Thinker				
Negative Thinker				
Lazy				
Hard-Working				
Introvert				
Shy				
Outgoing				
Narcissist				
Uncaring				

 # Notes

_____

_____

_____

_____

_____

_____

_____

_____

_____

_____

3 THE TRIANGLES OF LIFE

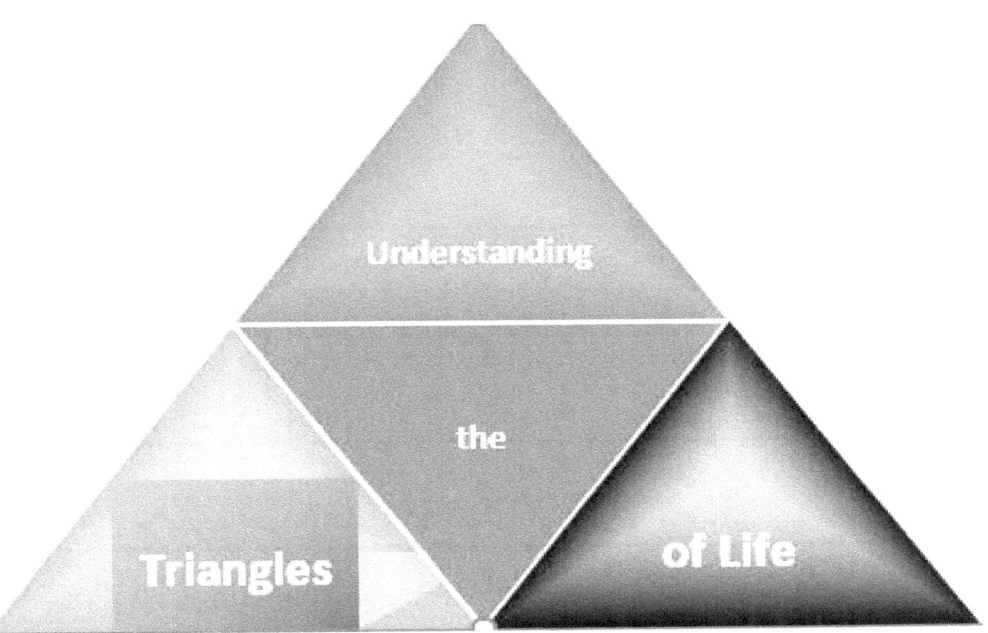

- The Brain
- The Philosophy of the Triangle
- The Self Triangle—Mind, Body, and Soul
- The Lifeline Triangle
- The Physical Needs Triangle
- The Emotional Needs Triangle
- Unstable/Broken Triangles
- Understanding Emotional Intelligence
- Threats to a Healthy Triangle—Drug Addiction, Alcohol, Tobacco, Anger, Stress

 # Notes

_____

_____

_____

_____

_____

_____

_____

_____

_____

_____

► THE BRAIN ◄

The brain is the center of all of a human being's physical and mental activities. Without its function, we either die or live in a state of unconsciousness.

The brain acts as the body's personal computer. It tells our body what to do; it communicates the body's needs; it formulates our thoughts; and it is where our intellectual and creative thoughts reside.

Lobes are associated with the largest part of the human brain called the cerebrum. There are four sections of the lobes.

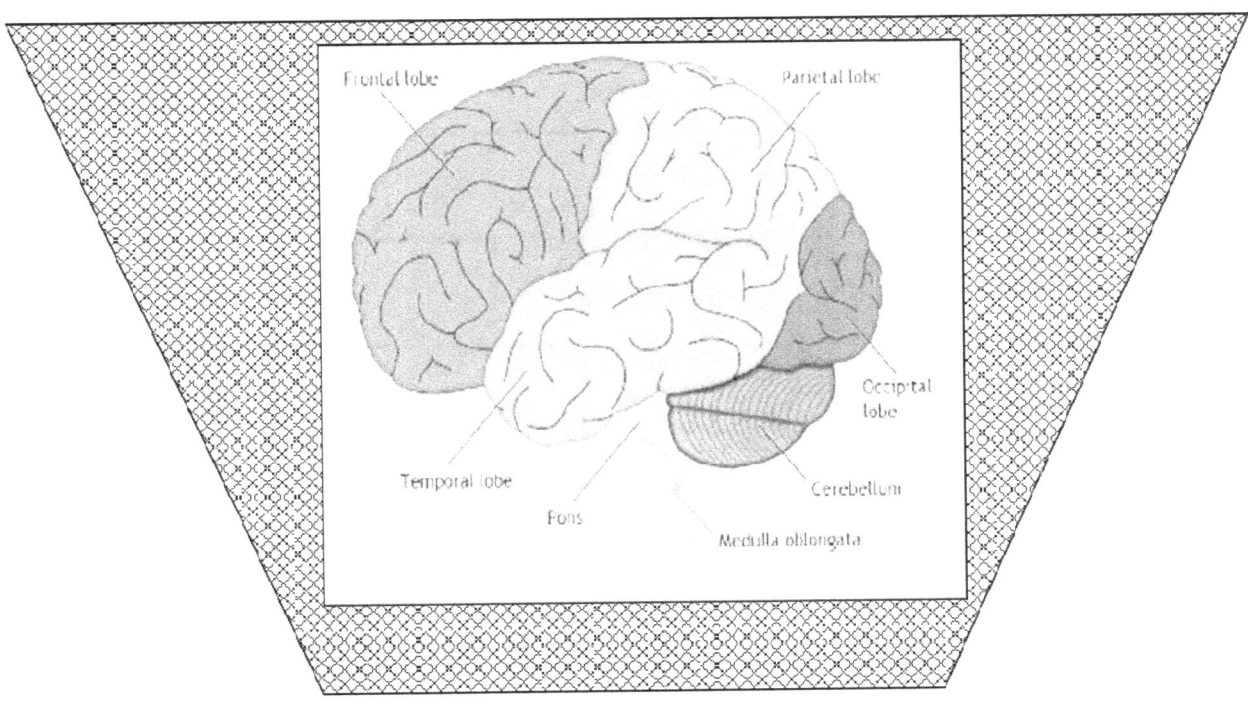

Parietal Lobe: Associated with movement, orientation, recognition, perception stimuli.

Occipital Lobe: Associated with visual processing.

Temporal Lobe: Associated with perception and recognition, auditory stimuli, memory and speech.

Frontal Lobe: Associated with reasoning, planning speech, movement, emotions and problem solving.

 # Notes

_____

_____

_____

_____

_____

_____

_____

_____

_____

_____

Clearly, as one can see, the brain plays a tremendous role in the state of our mental wellness. Knowledge is the nourishment that keeps the brain healthy and functioning properly. Rest, diet, and plenty of water is very important to the health of the brain. Exercise is good for the mind, because it produces serotonin. Serotonin is a mood regulator. The more we experience an upbeat mood, the more sound our mind.

► THE MIND ◄

"A mind is a terrible thing to waste."
The United Negro College Fund

The human mind, by definition, is that part of a human being that thinks, feels, and wills. It is our intellect and reason which allows us to navigate our way in this process we call life. The mind is constantly at work either consciously or unconsciously. The information our minds takes in during our early development can have an effect on the decisions we make as adults.

 # Notes

_____

_____

_____

_____

_____

_____

_____

_____

_____

_____

►Conquest for the Human Mind◄

There will always be forces competing for the minds of human beings. The most dominant of those forces today reside in popular culture. They consist of what I like to call the three M's: Media, Music, and Movies.

An example of this can be witnessed in our youth today and their following of hip-hop culture. Many of our young people today get their values from hip-hop and rap music. From the way that they dress to the way that they speak, this has had negative effects on our culture today.

In its inception, hip-hop music educated people to African American culture and reflected the injustices that existed in African American communities. When rap music started to reflect money, sex, and materialism in its lyrical content, it started to go global. It was a deliberate plan to dumb down the youth with this music by the powers that be.

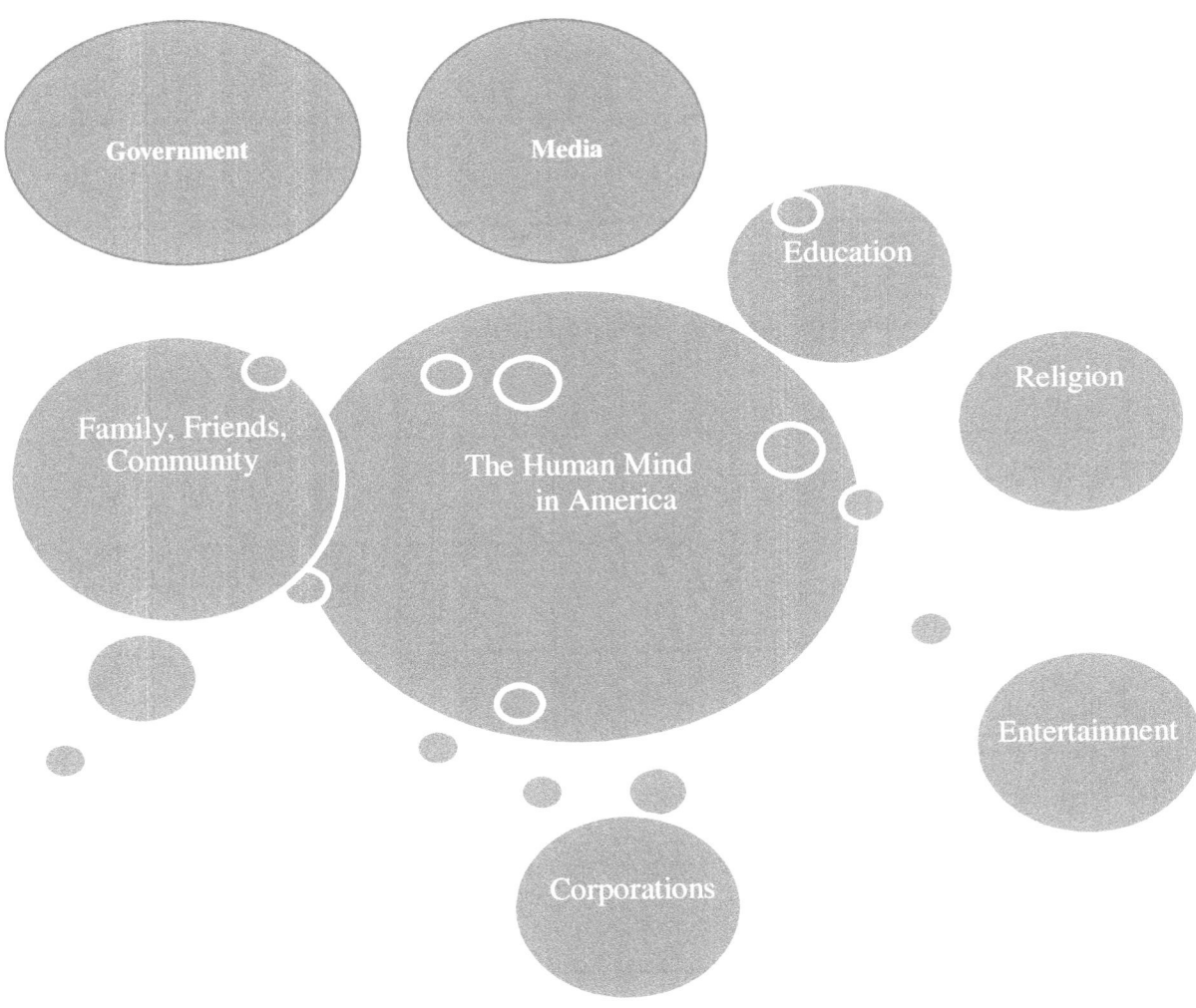

 # Notes

_____

_____

_____

_____

_____

_____

_____

_____

_____

_____

Reality television has such a profound impact on the way that people view entertainment, that reality tv shows are some of the most popular programming on television. Politicians often use slick commercials to influence people to vote for them.

Corrupt leaders use brainwashing as a means for controlling human beings. An example of this is used in the movie, "Conan the Barbarian" when one of the main characters, Thulsa Doom, played by James Earl Jones, explained to Conan, played by Arnold Schwarzenegger, this type of power.

Conan: You killed my mother! You killed my father! You killed my people! You took my father's sword.

Thusla Doom: Ah. It must have been when I was younger. There was a time, boy, when I searched for steel, when steel meant more to me than gold or jewels.

Conan: The riddle of steel.

Thusla Doom: Yes! You know what it is about, don't you, boy? Shall I tell you? It's the least I can do. Steel isn't strong, flesh is stronger! Look around you. There on the rock is a beautiful girl. Come to me my child.

Coaxes the girl to jump to her death.

That's strength! That's power! If power is the ability to control the minds of other people, then being the master of your own mind, is the greatest form of empowerment.

Empowerment comes from knowledge. Knowledge is the key. Frederick Douglass, the famed abolitionist and former slave acquired his freedom by knowledge. Like the body, the mind is fed a diet of information.

Knowledge is the most powerful form of information to feed the mind. The mind is also fed by life experiences as well as its relationship with other human beings. Step 3 of the 5 Step Plan delves into the power of knowledge and the different forms of knowledge.

 # Notes

_____

_____

_____

_____

_____

_____

_____

_____

_____

_____

The most dangerous thing to feed the mind is ignorance! Ignorance is responsible for all forms of self-destruction. The only people who benefit from ignorance are those who profit from it.

Ignorance is pervasive throughout our society. Knowledge must be sought out and is there if you choose to open your eyes and ears. The hardest part is the desire to seek it. If you seek it in small portions, the desire to seek more becomes addictive.

The film actress Diahann Carrol was once asked why she married a man so many years younger than she was and she responded by saying that he had such a brilliant mind, that he was wise beyond his years.

With a good mind comes a great imagination and with a great imagination comes innovation. Feeding the mind stimulates growth. Knowledge is the wings that give you a smooth journey throughout your life and when turbulence occurs, you are better equipped to navigate yourself through it.

A mind that is undeveloped will manifest itself in ignorant behavior. A mind that is not educated will become stagnant. A stagnant mind becomes a poisoned mind, which leads to poverty, crime, drug addiction, and other social ills that plague...........................

 # Notes

_____

_____

_____

_____

_____

_____

_____

_____

_____

_____

►The Body◄

"To have a sharp mind and an unfit body is a human contradiction."
—Rossi Turner, Professor

The health of our bodies plays an essential role in determining our quality of life. How we take care of our bodies is critical to our very survival. If we take a car, for example, we can see how good maintenance of a vehicle is very similar to good health, maintenance of our bodies. Many elderly people will take better care of their vehicle than younger people will. They make sure the vehicle has regular oil changes, they will have quarterly vehicle maintenance inspections, and more importantly, they will put less stress on a vehicle which will prolong the life of the vehicle.

Driving fast puts stress on the engine, transmission, and brakes of a vehicle. A vehicle can sustain high mileage if it is properly cared for, and driven at moderate speed. The language that I used to describe the proper maintenance of a vehicle is similar to the instructions a health care provider will give to their patient. What will a

 # Notes

_____

_____

_____

_____

_____

_____

_____

_____

_____

_____

good healthcare provider normally tell their patient?

Maintain a healthy diet, exercise in moderation, drink plenty of water, reduce stress, and avoid tobacco and alcohol. If you try to live a lifestyle as healthy as you possibly can, then being successful in the game of life will become simpler.

Examples of a healthy diet:

1. Choose good carbohydrates: whole grains, vegetables, fruits, and beans.
2. Stay away from foods high in sugar content.
3. Eat colorful fruits and vegetables.
4. Limit salt intake.
5. Drink plenty of water.
6. Take a multivitamin.
7. Eat whole grains.
8. Eat foods with calcium.
9. Eat healthy fats such as nuts and fish.
10. Eat poultry and chicken.
11. Limit meats as much as possible.

Examples of moderate exercises:
1. Brisk walking
2. Bicycling
3. Yard work such as mowing the lawn
4. Water aerobics
5. Jump roping
6. Hitting a boxing bag in moderation
7. Planks for abdominal muscles

 # Notes

_____

_____

_____

_____

_____

_____

_____

_____

_____

_____

►The Soul◄

Soul: Relates to the spiritual part of a person. It is the essence of who we are that excludes the physical part of a person. The soul is everlasting. Even as the physical body dies, the soul lives, according to those who believe in the creator of the human, heavens, and the earth. The soul defines our beliefs, our morals, and values. The soul of a person is as unique to an individual as a fingerprint.

What makes us unique from all other living things is our ability to have guilt, or be tormented. A healthy soul means being at peace with oneself. I have listed means that will achieve this:

1. Ask forgiveness for those you have injured.

2. Try to rectify the wrongs you have omitted.

3. Expand your knowledge to expand your morals.
   Example: Expanding your morals will enable you to expand your moral consciousness.

4. Work to make yourself a better human being by respecting others.

5. Learn to love yourself.

 # Notes

_____

_____

_____

_____

_____

_____

_____

_____

_____

6. Want for your fellow human being what you would want for yourself.

7. Be aware of your weaknesses. Acknowledge them and attempt to correct them.

►The Philosophy of the Triangles◄

In my seventeen years of social work, I have seen human beings struggle to overcome conditions of poverty, neglect, and abuse. It pains me to say, that in many cases, I have worked or bear witness to, many of these individuals or families that remained trapped in the vicious cycles of marginalization. After much thought and analysis of their social plights, I came up with the theory I call "The Triangles of Life."

 # Notes

_____

_____

_____

_____

_____

_____

_____

_____

_____

_____

The Triangles of Life Consist of Four Triangles:

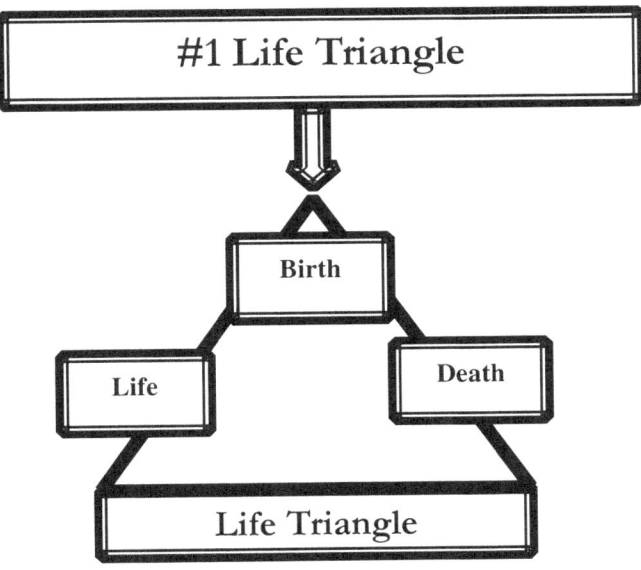

As mentioned in the beginning of the book "The Game of Life Concept" each human being is dealt a hand of cards which they have absolutely no choice of the cards dealt to them. No human being comes into this world with their choice in a number of things. The most obvious of course are:

Who their parents will be
What their race will be
What their economic status will be
What their gender will be
What their ethnicity will be
What their physical features will be
Will they be have physical or mental handicaps

Race, gender, cultural heritage, and economies determined the cards a person is throughout their lives. Poverty is a perfect example of this. Poverty is more often than not generational and this is a direct result of poor people being dealt cards that keep them mired in poverty. The wealthy on the other hand are dealt cards that not only maintain their wealth but increase it.

 Notes

_____

_____

_____

_____

_____

_____

_____

_____

_____

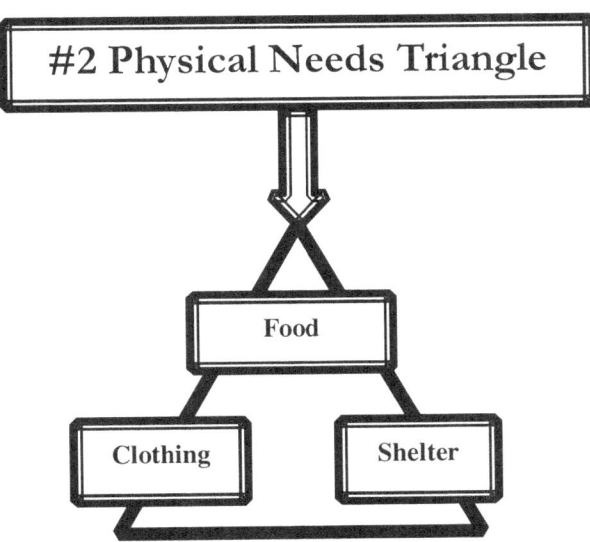

Food, clothing, and shelter are three things humans need for survival. These primitive needs are the very essence of our survival on earth. The struggle to maintain our physical needs triangle is something that the majority of the people on this earth deal with on a day to day basis. It takes either wealth, employment that pays a living wage or skills and talent which the public is willing to pay for, in order to sustain our physical needs triangle.

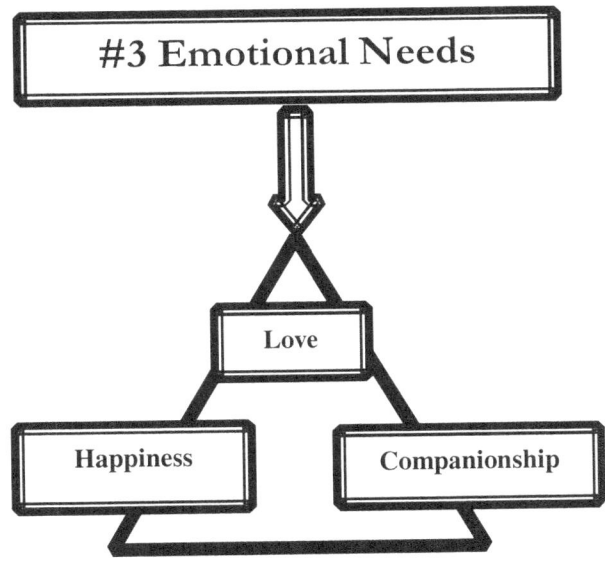

 # Notes

_____

_____

_____

_____

_____

_____

_____

_____

_____

_____

Companionship is an essential need of human beings. It's proven that when people have strong relationships where love is present, it sustains the very essence of our being. Healthy relationships means healthy people. Relationships are also necessary for securing and maintaining our physical needs. Through our relationships, families are developed and communities are established. Working together with other people strengthens bonds that allows us security in the maintaining of our physical needs. Our desire for love, happiness, and companionship is innate in all human beings.

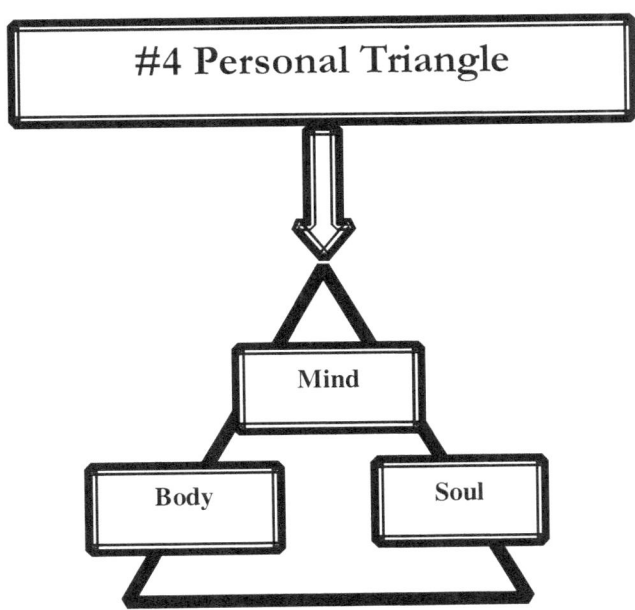

The personal triangle is the essence of who we are as individuals. The mind consists of our intellect, which is key to our survival. With a sharp mind comes wisdom, common sense, and the ability to be rational and reasonable. Our minds are enhanced by the seeking of knowledge. The mind is what helps us with our tools for survival. The body is the physical structure of a human being. Our survival also requires the body to be strong and healthy in order to sustain our physical needs. This was especially true during earlier times when hunting, farming, and building was necessary for our food, clothing, and shelter.

The soul is our morals, values, and ethics as an individual. Most individuals believe our soul is connected to our spirituality which is our belief in a higher being greater than ourselves. Actually what makes belief in a supreme being so comforting is that all of our needs in the highest of form are guaranteed if we obey the rule and beliefs required by the article of faith.

There can be no survival without a high set of morals, values, and ethics. It is also true that when people live with substandard physical needs and emotional needs, it has an adverse effect on their mind, body, and soul.

 # Notes

_____

_____

_____

_____

_____

_____

_____

_____

_____

_____

►Government, Corporations and the Triangles of Life◄

As our lives become more dependent on the government and businesses for sustaining our physical needs triangle, our emotional needs triangle has become less important. There was a time when societies were agrarian and the need for people working together to secure our physical needs were essential. This in turn bonded people together emotionally.

With the advancement of technology, people began to search for opportunities that required them to move to different parts of the country and the world. Families become estranged due to these advancements in technology. People have thus become indoctrinated in the philosophy of individual good over the overall good of family and community.

This along with the changing social norms began to tear at the fabric of the emotional needs triangle. Personal independence and self-gratification became the mindset of people. See the diagram below:

Personal ambitions over Cooperation

Self-Indulgence over Sacrifice

Me over Us

Getting in touch with oneself over Connecting with others

Personal Happiness over Compassion for others and our children

The results of this is a total breakdown in the emotional needs triangle.
The weakening of the emotional triangles has contributed to many in the society, to fall through the cracks of hopelessness and despair.

 # Notes

_____

_____

_____

_____

_____

_____

_____

_____

_____

_____

►Understanding Emotional Intelligence◄

Emotional Intelligence is the ability to control, understand, use, and manage your emotions in positive ways to relieve stress, communicate effectively, empathize with others, overcome challenges, and defuse conflict.

Emotional Intelligence enables you to recognize our own emotional state, and the emotional state of others. You are able to relate better to people and engage with them; that draws them to you.

Emotional Intelligence allows you to accomplish goals easier, because you are able to reason and encourage people to assist you with your agenda.

Emotional Intelligence consists of four attributes:

SELF-AWARENESS:
Recognize your emotions.
Know your strengths and weaknesses.

SELF-MANAGEMENT:
Control your impulse feelings, manage your behavior, and adapt to change, follow through on commitments.

SOCIAL AWARENESS:
Understand the emotions, needs, and concerns of others.

RELATIONSHIP MANAGEMENT:
Know how to develop and maintain good relationships, communicate clearly and manage conflict.

 # Notes

_____

_____

_____

_____

_____

_____

_____

_____

_____

_____

►Example of Emotional Intelligence◄

Muhammad Ali was the master of emotional intelligence in the boxing ring. An example of this took place during his preparation for his fight with George Foreman for the heavyweight championship of the world. Ali, himself, said that he wondered how hard Foreman hit. Although he never admitted this publicly, I believe Ali was dealing with his own fears of the unknown. How hard does he hit? Can I take his punch?

As a person who has been a part of boxing, I know the most common emotions are fear and doubt. Another emotion that can be just as bad is over-confidence. Ali decided to attack Foreman verbally. He would stand up to him and ridicule his lack

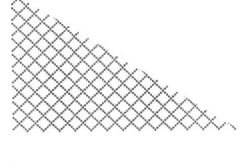

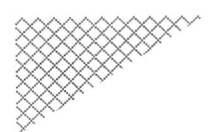

of boxing skills. He would tell anyone listening that he was the scientific boxer. He had experience. Foreman has never gone the distance. By saying this, Ali was not only psyching Foreman out, but psyching himself as well.

There were two prominent emotions in the Ali-Foreman fight—fear and over-confidence. Foreman had no doubt in his mind that he would destroy Ali. He later admitted his fear of Joe Frazier and Ken Norton, both of whom he knocked out. Ali, on the other hand, posed no threat in Foreman's mind.

Overconfidence and confidence played a major role in the outcome of the fight. Foreman entered the ring totally convinced he would knock Ali out between first and third rounds. Ali with his fertile mind employed the rope-a-dope designed to get Foreman to punch himself out. As the fight went by, Ali's confidence grew and Foreman's began to wane.

The result was Ali by a knockout. Ali shocked the world once again as he beat a man that was just as feared as the man Ali beat the first time he won the title ten years earlier—Sonny Liston. What Ali had that made him a great champion was, of course, the obvious—talent, heart, determination, and a high boxing IQ.

George Foreman, at the time, was one of the most imposing, hard-hitting, and formidable heavyweight champions. His opponents were so frightened of him that they lost before they stepped in the ring. The emotion of fear so overwhelmed them that they would fall to the canvas without being hit hard.

Ali had to overcome his own fears and doubts. He had to overcome fear on the part of his trainers. Ali's first order of business was to agitate and talk about Fore-

 # Notes

_____

_____

_____

_____

_____

_____

_____

_____

_____

_____

man. He saw Foreman in Jack Dempsey's restaurant and walked to where Foreman was standing with a former great champion, Jack Dempsey. Ali told Foreman that he was not a champ; he was a chump. I whipped Sonny Liston (former champion Ali beat when he was young—who was equally—if not more frightening), and I'll whip you. Foreman walked out, and Ali winked to Dempsey and said, "I just won the first round."

To the average person, why would Ali make someone as big and strong as George Foreman angry? Was Ali being overly emotional? In fact, Ali was using psychological warfare. Ali had rationally concluded that if you stand up to a bully and act crazy and unafraid, the bully will be afraid. It also helped him overcome his own fears. George had scared his other opponents by scaring them to death before they got into the ring, and knocking them out after they stepped into the ring.

Ali already had his strategy. He would hit Foreman at the beginning ring and stay away by boxing. At the beginning of the bell, Ali did just that. He ran out and hit Foreman in the nose, and started dancing around, and noticed Foreman was matching him step for step.

Ali, at that moment, realized that it would be him and not Foreman who would be exhausted. Ali changed his game plan and went to the ropes. Ali allowed Foreman to pound on his body. Ali kept talking, "George, who told you that you hit hard? Is that all you got, George?" This talk would infuriate George Foreman, and he would swing harder at Ali's body, with Ali blocking most of those shots with his arms. Before the end of each round, Ali would hit Foreman with four or five punch combinations. By the eighth round, Foreman was so exhausted that he got knocked out by Ali. Ali shocked the world once again.

> Let's look at this as an exercise on how Ali used his mind to beat one of the most imposing boxers of his time.

How was Ali able to use his mind to beat a younger and harder hitting boxer than himself?

What were the two prominent emotions of this fight?

How did emotions play a role in the fight?

 # Notes

_____

_____

_____

_____

_____

_____

_____

_____

_____

_____

►My Analysis◄

Ali had to psych himself out to face George Foreman. Two opponents who had beaten Ali – Joe Frazier and Ken Norton – were knocked out easily by Foreman. Ali did manage to avenge his two losses, but both were by decisions. Foreman had been built up as the hardest-hitting heavyweight champion of all time. He was feared in much the same as Sonny Liston before him (whom Ali beat) and Mike Tyson (after him). Ali did what he had done ten years earlier with Sonny Liston. He overcame his initial fear of his opponent to plot a strategy for victory.

►Threats to a Healthy Triangle◄

Drug Addiction

The brain is the most important organ in the healthy triangle. When the brain is threatened, then the healthy triangle is at risk. Drug addiction can do irreparable harm to a healthy triangle, thereby reducing one's quality of life. To engage in illegal or legal drug use and abuse have serious consequences to your health and to the lives of those closest to you.

Each part of the brain has a specific job. Earlier in step two of this program, I discussed the functioning of these brain parts. Drugs are chemicals that are put into the body by injecting, inhaling, smoking, or eating them. They affect the way our communication signals work in the brain.

We have a chemical in our brains called dopamine. Dopamine is a neurotransmitter that affects mood, attitude, and motivation. The brain also has serotonin. Serotonin regulates emotions, and regulates sleep and appetite. Exercise can produce serotonin. When our bodies are in pain, our brain produces endorphins.

Drugs such as opioids, heroin, and other pain medications can disrupt the natural chemical processes in our brains. Opiates can release 2-10 times the amount of dopamine our brains will naturally produce.

To use an example of how this works, what does a person do when the music on a stereo is too loud? They turn it down. Well, the brain does the same thing when it is flooded with too much dopamine. Your brain adjusts itself accordingly by producing less dopamine.

Once your body produces less dopamine and less serotonin, you become physi-

 # Notes

_____

_____

_____

_____

_____

_____

_____

_____

_____

_____

cally sick. You become depressed, anxious, nervous and unable to enjoy things that normally brought you pleasure. Now, the quest to get that almighty high begins. Changes in your look and behavior will become more pronounced. The gradualism will take on a horrific effect to those who knew you before your addiction.

I liken it to the movie "The Exorcist" in which the little girl was possessed by the demon. The demon had invaded the girl but didn't fully manifest itself until later on when it had complete control of her body and mind. By that time her body and personality made such a horrific change that her own mother told the priest, "That thing upstairs is not my daughter." The priest and his fellow senior priest knew that in order to save the little girl and drive the demon out, they had to wage war against the demon.

The little girl had the two priests to help drive the demon from her soul. She couldn't do it alone. There was a touching scene in the movie when the little girl was not under the grip of the beast. The demon was at rest. The girl wrote a message to the priest from her soul on her stomach—Help me! The priest knew what he had to do!

He received permission from the cardinal to perform the exorcism. The priest was assigned an experienced wiser priest to lead the exorcism. The older priest warned the young priest as they prepared to do battle with the demon to "avoid conversation." To ask what is relevant is okay, but anything beyond that is not. "The beast is a liar, but he will also mix the truth with lies. The attack is psychological and dangerous—so do not listen."

As bad as this analogy may sound to someone, it is about the same torture that an addict goes through. To people who have loved ones with addiction, the descriptions are nearly the same, except the demon is drugs or alcohol. The only difference is the addict has to fight this battle alone. There are support groups, but the battle is an internal battle. You against the drug!

In the early stages of addiction, when it's not in full effect, it is difficult to recognize the addiction and then acknowledge that you have an addiction. It's easier to fight it if you can catch it early. The key is recognition of the addiction and acknowledging that you are an addict. The last thing in the early stage is the desire to quit. Once the desire to quit is there, then you refer back to Point 1 Who Are You, and start from there.

The worst, and by far the hardest, form of drug addiction to fight is full-blown addiction. In this form of addiction, the drug has completely taken over your triangle—mind, body, and soul. Your body is sick without the drug, and your soul has become dormant. At the weakest point, the addict knows they have to exorcise the demon from the mind and body.

The first step in doing this is simple—yet so hard. It is simply making up your mind to do it. Once the desire to quit is stronger than the desire to use, the process of taking that first step on the road to emancipation begins.

 # Notes

_____

_____

_____

_____

_____

_____

_____

_____

_____

_____

Alcohol

Alcohol is classified as a drug. Alcohol has many ingredients that make it poisonous to our bodies. Negative long-term effects are catastrophic to your health. Alcohol creates temporary damage to your vital organs such as your kidney, liver, brain, pancreas, and the other central nervous system. The liver is the organ most affected by alcohol consumption.

What is alcohol? Alcohol is made by germs that come from yeast. They work in juices of grapes and other fruits when pressed out and allowed to stay in a warm place. The germs live and grow on the sugar in juices which produce alcohol. When the ingredients ferment, alcohol is produced. What makes alcohol dangerous is that one can develop an addiction to alcohol. Once this occurs, the body comes to depend on the alcohol. The process of possession takes place.

Alcohol can cause serious damage to the brain. Alcohol dulls the senses and weakens the brain. The ability to control or restrain one's emotions becomes severely challenged. Alcohol dulls a person's ability to think quickly or rationally. Alcohol not only affects you physically, but it affects your personal life.

Tobacco/Cigarettes

Tobacco is dangerous for many reasons, but by far the most damaging is the 4,000 chemicals in cigarettes. Fifty-one of them are carcinogenic. A carcinogen is something that causes cancer. Some of the chemicals found in cigarettes are:

Carbon monoxide which is found in car exhausts
Nicotine which is found in bug sprays
Arsenic which is found in rat poison
Hydrogen cyanide which is a poisonous gas

The most widely known chemical that most people are familiar with is nicotine. Nicotine is a strong poisonous drug that is used in pesticides and bug sprays. Besides cancer, cigarettes can cause emphysema and heart disease. Cigarettes are also costly. A pack of cigarettes can cost $5.00 or more per pack. (Source: History of Tobacco Health Literacy)

 # Notes

_____

_____

_____

_____

_____

_____

_____

_____

_____

_____

Anger

In the movie "The Godfather," the patriarch Don Corleone had three sons: Sonny, Fredo, and Michael. Sonny, the oldest, had a hot temper, and his hot temper led him to be killed because his enemies knew this and set him up. Uncontrolled anger produces uncontrolled behavior, which leads to regretful actions. See Anger Report Card

Anger Report Card (ARC)
What triggers your anger?
1. Is your anger uncontrollable?
2. Are you harboring any anger?
3. Has your anger cost you anything?
4. Does fear trigger your anger?
5. Have you tried to manage your anger?
6. Can you control your anger?

Stress

Stress is a part of our daily lives. The important thing is understanding what stress is. Stress is an important and necessary physical reaction in our body's response to harmful situations. When a person feels a threat, a chemical reaction occurs in the body that allows a person to react in order to prevent injury. This reaction is called "fight or flight," also known as the stress response.

During this stress response, your muscles tighten, your blood pressure rises; your heart rate speeds up, and your breathing becomes rapid. Your body is now ready to act in order to protect itself.

People are different and so is their ability to deal with stress. What can be highly stressful to one person can be of little concern to another person. Our bodies are not conditioned to deal with high levels of stress constantly. Living with stress is likened to driving a car full throttle for a long period of time—eventually something has to give.

The emotional symptoms from stress are: irritability, depression, feeling the

 # Notes

_____

_____

_____

_____

_____

_____

_____

_____

_____

_____

loss of control, difficulty relaxing, loss of self-esteem, and self-isolation.

The physical symptoms from stress are: headaches, stomach pains, aches and muscle pains, chest pains, colds, insomnia, no longer receiving pleasure in things that were once enjoyable.

Stress Report Card

Do you get stressed easily?

Does stress trigger destructive behavior?

How does stress affect your physical health?

How does stress affect your mental health?

Does the fast pace of life stress you?

Do finances stress you?

Do certain associations stress you?

Examples of Reducing Stress

Set Realistic Goals—If goals are set unrealistically high, it can produce unnecessary stress.

Prioritize Your Life—Have your priorities in order. In other words, pay your bills before you go on that vacation cruise.

Eliminate Emotional Users—These are friends and associates who only call when they need help.

Take Walks—Walking can ease the stress levels by increasing serotonin.

Organize Your Life—Keep a planner and follow it religiously.

Prayer or Meditation

Get Your Rest

 # Notes

_____

_____

_____

_____

_____

_____

_____

_____

_____

_____

4 THE POWER OF KNOWLEDGE

- Power
- Power Through Mind Control
- Knowledge
- Knowledge Is the Key to Human Development
- Decision-Making Enhancement
- Characteristics of Developed and Undeveloped

Power

Power is sought more than anything in the history of humanity. It has been the cause of more human atrocities than anything in world history. Power is more seductive than sex; it is craved more than food. People have killed each other for power; countries have fought wars for power.

There is not one institution in any form of business, government, civic, or community where someone does not crave being number one. In sports those with the most talent have more power than those who are less talented. Teams with a tradition of winning have more prestige, wealth, and power than small market teams with losing traditions. For example, the New York Yankees is the most powerful team in Major League Baseball.

 # Notes

_____

_____

_____

_____

_____

_____

_____

_____

_____

_____

Although all of the teams are part of the same organization and are considered equal, the Yankees are first among equals. Two of the most obvious forms of power are money and political power. Money is the greatest instrument of power in the world because all societies depend on currency to purchase a person's basic needs. The more money you have the more you are able to secure those needs.

If you are rich, however, money takes on an entirely different level. When a person is flushed with cash, he or she can buy access to political power. They can coerce politicians and community leaders into doing things against the best interest of those they have sworn to serve.

People have turned on their own family members over money. Money is the strongest driving force for most of the ills of our societies. Political power is the most sought after power institutionally.

Political power is craved because through politics you can control the lives of millions of people. An example of this type of power is the power of Mayor Richard J. Daley. Major Daily had such a formidable political machine in the city of Chicago that nothing of significance could happen in the city of Chicago without his approval.

What makes a person with political power so unique is the leadership of government institutions.

People depend on the government for acquiring their basic needs of food, shelter, and clothing. Controlling a person's mind is by far the most dangerous form of power. This type of power makes its victim do and support things against their own best interest.

People under the spell of this type of power have the most difficult time overcoming obstacles because their mind is not their own.

 # Notes

_____

_____

_____

_____

_____

_____

_____

_____

_____

_____

Diagram of Power

Fear, Bullying, and Peer Pres-	Charismatic Leadership
Television, music, and movies	Ignorance, Lies, and Miseduca-

Charismatic Leadership: Charismatic leaders have had much sway on the thinking of people. The one thing these leaders have in common is their ability to use the gift of oratory to amass followers. Here again, it is in religion and politics where you usually find this type of leader.

Leaders with good intentions and a righteous cause can be a force of good. Martin Luther King is a perfect example of a leader who was a gifted orator and highly intelligent. He put his life on the line to liberate people from the shackles of oppression. Adolf Hitler on the other hand used his oratory and leadership abilities as a means to gain power and commit horrific crimes against Jewish people.

Most people are followers of something or someone. The most important thing to remember is to think for yourself. If you choose to support your mind and your eyes are wide open, knowledge is the key to doing this.

Ignorance, Lies and Miseducation: Keeping people ignorant is essential to control. Ignorance is the psychological means that keep people shackled in oppression, exploitation, and inhumanity. Miseducation is another form of controlling what people think.

Dr. Carter G. Woodson, the African American historian and founder of Black History wrote in his book *The Miseducation of the Negro* that, "If you can control a man's thinking, you won't have to tell him to go to the back door, and he will automatically go there. If there is no back door he will create one."

Lies are another form of mind control. The lie is dangerous because the liar is trying to persuade you to believe something that is not true. There are times a person will lie to protect himself or someone else. However, lying can lead to more lies, and the next thing you know, you are living a lie. Once this happens, the stress and guilt will begin to take its toll. The liar will begin to believe his own lies, making ref-

Notes

_____

_____

_____

_____

_____

_____

_____

_____

_____

_____

ormation of himself impossible. It is like telling yourself you are not an alcoholic, and the truth is that you are.

Fear, Bullying, and Peer Pressure: Fear is the option that is used to control. In the movie "A Bronx Tale," the young man asked a mobster if it is better to be feared or loved. The mobster said it would be nice to be both, but if he had his choice, he would rather be feared.

Fear freezes its victim into doing nothing to overcome their plight. It is fear that prevents people from acting in their best interest. Fear keeps people from trying to do things that will make their lives better. Fear keeps people from fighting against oppression and injustice.

Bullying is important to mention because the person who is being victimized is allowing the victimizer to control them psychologically. Bullying is seeking power and control to cover up their own fears and sense of inadequacies.

Peer pressure can be very similar in that people often do things they don't want to do because of peer pressure. There is the fear of not being accepted by the majority. People who get hooked on drugs and alcohol often do so because of peer pressure. However, there can be nothing more liberating than doing what is right when it is more popular to do what is wrong.

Television, Music, and Movies: There is a name given to television by those critical of television, and its effects on people—the idiot box. I'm quite sure those who make their living in television would find offense to this term. However, the name is deserving. Most adults watch television 20 to 25 hours a week. Children watch television, in some cases, over 40 hours a week. Most of the programming promotes buffoonery.

Reality television is based on shows that feature little if any redeeming values. Shows such as "How to Marry a Millionaire," "The Housewives of Beverly Hills," which is a spinoff from the sitcom "Beverly Hills Housewives, "Honey Boo Boo," and other reality shows with huge ratings but have nothing in the way of wisdom.

Entertainment provides us with programming that appeals to our lust for materialism, wealth, and sex. Instead of art reflecting our higher selves as people, it reflects buffoonery that people act out in their daily lives.

 # Notes

_____

_____

_____

_____

_____

_____

_____

_____

_____

_____

Knowledge

Knowledge is defined by the Oxford English Dictionary as expertise and skills acquired by a person through experience or education; the theoretical or practical understanding of a subject.

Knowledge is power! It is the great equalizer. It is the liberator of injustice and the champion of freedom. Knowledge is the light that provides the vision in a world of darkness. There is no freedom without knowledge.

It is the human being's nature to seek knowledge. This is because human beings need food, shelter, and clothing for survival. In order to secure and maintain these basic needs, humans had to learn their environment. It was through observation, investigation, and trial and error that humans began to acquire knowledge of their surroundings.

Humans began to understand the patterns of weather and called it seasons. They observed the benefits from the rain. They discovered that there is a difference in water: the oceans had salt water and the rivers and streams had fresh water that could be used for drinking.

Seeking knowledge allowed the human being to enhance his life on earth. The power of knowledge is so great that Socrates is quoted to have said, "The only good is knowledge, and the only evil is ignorance."

When a person has hit rock bottom due to drugs, alcohol, unemployment, or life itself—it is knowledge that is the ladder out of the hole. Knowledge is the road to emancipation. It opens the mind up to unlimited possibilities.

If knowledge is the light, then ignorance is the darkness. The only people who benefit from ignorance are those who profit from it; otherwise, ignorance is found in every social ill of the world. Poor people are the biggest sufferers from ignorance because forces in society have either consciously or subconsciously kept them there. Ignorance is not just an issue with the poor. People of economic classes suffer from ignorance. Poor people are just shackled to their impoverished conditions due to ignorance.

 # Notes

_____

_____

_____

_____

_____

_____

_____

_____

_____

_____

Knowledge is the Key to Human Development

►Terms to Know◄

Common Sense: The ability to perceive, understand and judge things shared by nearly all people.

Wisdom: The ability to think and act using knowledge, experience, understanding, common sense, and insight.

Vision: The act or power of predicting that which has yet to materialize. This requires a creative imagination.

Morals: A set of values and beliefs of an individual.

Ethics: A code of standards put forth by a society or cultural group.

Values: A personal fundamental belief or principle.

Life Experiences: Experiences that a person learns from life including: family, community, culture, and society.

Reasoning Skills: Reason or reasoning is associated with thinking, cognition, and intellect. Having good reasoning is having the ability to make sense of things by applying logic, establishing facts, and rendering sound decisions followed by correct action.

Moral Conscience: The inner voice which tells you whether your actions are good or bad, right or wrong.

 # Notes

_____

_____

_____

_____

_____

_____

_____

_____

_____

_____

Decision Making
Enhancement

Knowledge and Wisdom:
Knowledge is acquired
through a life of listening
and observation.

Morals and Values: Morals are a set of values
and beliefs that an individual has. Values are
a person's fundamental belief or principles

Common Sense and Critical Thinking: Common sense is the ability
to perceive, understand, and judge things shared by nearly all people. Critical thinking is the ability to identify a problem and come up
with a rational solution.

Decision making is what life is all about. Everyone has to make decisions. Good decisions can bring you a lifetime of rewards. Bad decisions can cause you a lifetime of misery. From the time we wake up until the time we go to bed our life is full of making decisions. Some decisions are built into the subconscious, such as getting up to go to work or school. Many of our decisions in life are institutional by nature. Therefore, much of what we do is based on instinct.

What is important about making sound decisions is realizing that your decisions can positively or adversely affect the lives of others. I can't tell you how many times I have talked to a young man and asked, "What were you thinking after killing another young man," and without fail, I am told, "I don't know what I was thinking."

This is why critical thinking is important. A person with limited knowledge is often a poor decision maker.

 # Notes

_____

_____

_____

_____

_____

_____

_____

_____

_____

_____

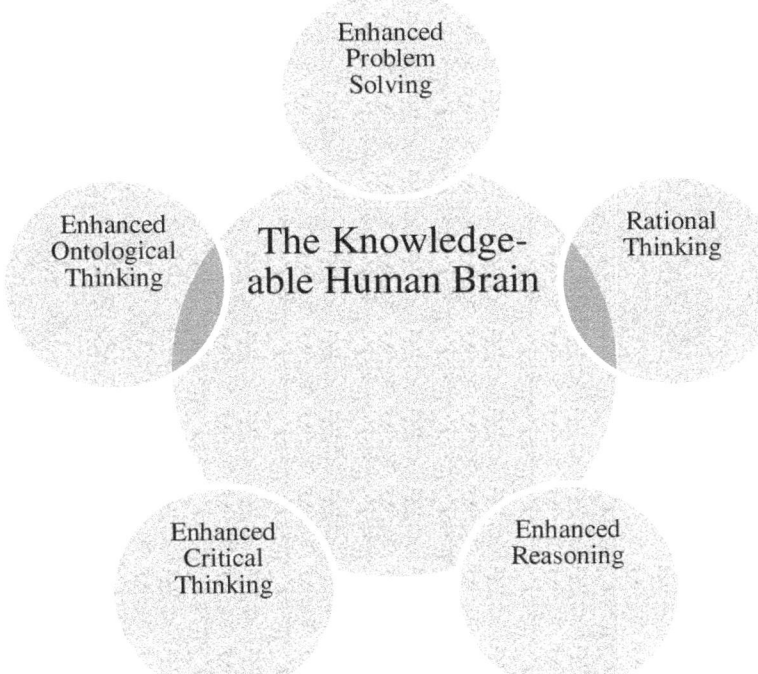

Characteristics of Developed and Undeveloped Human Beings

Developed people conduct themselves in a proper way both privately and publicly. This development is started early by their parents, guardians, other adults, and older children in the life of a child.

Developed Human Beings

- Determine right from wrong
- Expand their knowledge
- Build society
- Have a social and moral conscience

Undeveloped Human Beings
- Lifestyles and values are distorted
- Lack critical thinking skills

 # Notes

_____

_____

_____

_____

_____

_____

_____

_____

_____

_____

- Life is mere existence

What makes people undeveloped?
- Ignorance
- Too much entertainment (TV, video games)
- Lack of knowledge

Human development can be measured in four basic ways:

1. Physical: Nutrition and Exercise
2. Psychological: Nature and Nurture
3. Intellectual: Education, Participation, Observation
4. Moral: Religion, Society, Community, Family

The physical pertains to the body, while the psychological and intellectual pertains to the mind. Moral development pertains directly to the soul.

 # Notes

_____

_____

_____

_____

_____

_____

_____

_____

_____

_____

5 LESSONS FOR LIFE

- A Revolution of the Mind
- Men
- Women
- Children
- The Miracle of Life
- Poverty

A Revolution of the Mind

Revolutions are bloody; revolutions are ugly, but there are times that revolutions are necessary. Every day around the world, there are either revolutions or threats of revolution occurring. The United States was formed through revolution. Oppression and injustice are the seeds of revolution. Not all revolutions are about war and violent conflicts. There have been cultural revolutions in which the people demanded a change in the customs and mores of a country.

There was the industrial revolution in which new machinery changed the way goods were produced and labor was used. There have been revolutionary changes in technology, arts, and sports. Then there is a personal mental revolution. This occurs when an individual's life is so horrific that a radical way of thinking is necessary.

There has to be willingness to change. Change is very difficult for most people. Change requires reprogramming your thinking and adjusting your behavior. Behavioral adjustment is required when you are trying to emancipate from the shackles of hopelessness and stagnation.

 # Notes

_____

_____

_____

_____

_____

_____

_____

_____

_____

_____

I will relate a story of mental revolution from a young man I met when he was in prison. I was giving a motivational speech at a step-down prison in Tennessee. This particular young man was very attentive during the speech. He spoke with me and my colleague afterwards, and I remember being impressed with his intelligence. It was obvious that he was exceptional.

A few months later, I received a phone call from him asking me if I would come to his parole hearing. I, along with a colleague, went to the hearing. The parole board was very impressed with his presentation, and a few months later, he was re-leased. I ran into him about three or four months later at a neighborhood function and asked him how he was doing. He said that he was working as a barber but was having a difficult time seeking employment because of his prison record. I spoke with my colleague, and through his efforts, he was able to secure a job with our company through AmeriCorps. From there he began to shine.

Today, he works with a non-profit agency in which he heads a youth pro-gram. He was chosen for that position over people with master's degrees. I asked him once, what it was that changed his life. He said that while playing basketball in the prison yard, he decided that he didn't want to die in prison. From that moment on, he began to read and take advantage of programs in the prison. He was on his journey to the road to emancipation.

Knowledge was the road map to his journey. His revolutionary moment came on the basketball court in a state prison.

The price of revolution is costly, but the freedom is worth that price.

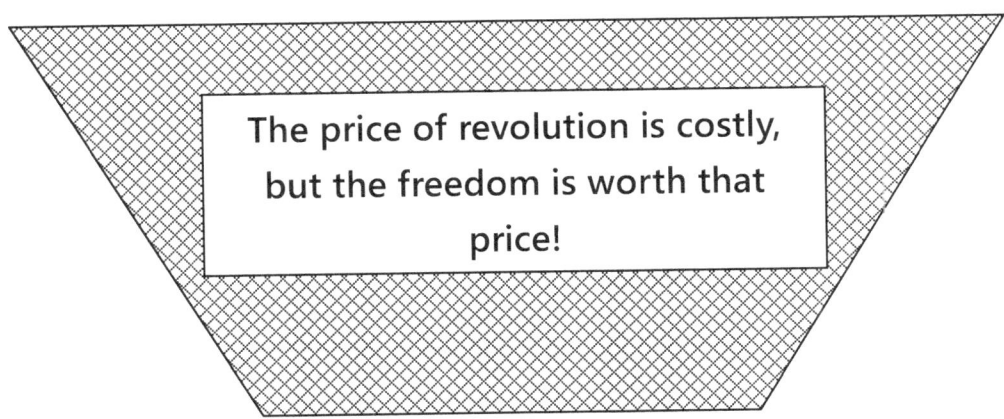

The price of revolution is costly, but the freedom is worth that price!

 # Notes

_____

_____

_____

_____

_____

_____

_____

_____

_____

CHILDREN

Children are our future, yet they are the most neglected and abused human beings on earth. The largest population of homeless people in America are children. The largest number of people living in poverty in America are children.

Our future as a human race depends on how our children's needs are provided.

Children Need

- Love
- Nurturing
- Direction
- Support
- Patience
- Positive Reinforcement
- Knowledge

Having children without providing for and securing their needs is hazardous to human survival.

 # Notes

_____

_____

_____

_____

_____

_____

_____

_____

_____

_____

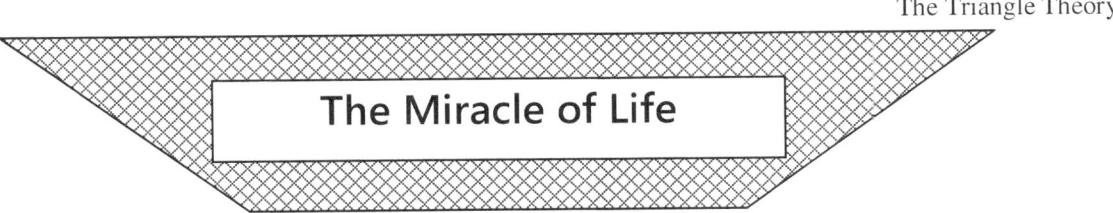

The Miracle of Life

►One in A Million You◄

"One in a Million You" is the title of Larry Graham's 1980 hit song. When we examine difficult problems in our lives, the odds seem so insurmountable, that to carry on in a positive manner seems useless. However, if we look at our journey to life, it was fraught with dangers and incredible odds, in which it took us to be born.

A pregnancy begins when a sperm fertilizes an egg as a man ejaculates semen containing millions of sperm. That sperm is deposited into the vagina, into the uterus, and then into the fallopian. Most sperm die along the way. In each tube, only a few thousand sperm the ampulla, a section that makes up one-half to two-thirds of the tube's length. If a sperm fertilizes an egg, it usually does so in the part of the ampulla near the uterus. Some sperm reach the fallopian tubes in as little as five minutes. Others take hours.

Sperm can survive in the fallopian tubes for up to 48 hours. It takes an egg 72 hours to pass through the fallopian tube. The egg can be fertilized only during the first 24 hours of this period. Therefore, intercourse must take place near the time of ovulation for fertilization to occur.

The surface of this newly released egg is covered with a jelly like layer of cells called zona pellucida. A second layer of cell, called the cumulus oophorus which surrounds the zona pellucida. A sperm must pass through both layers to fertilize the egg. The acrosome (tip) of the sperm releases special enzymes that scatter cells of both layers. Although several sperm may begin to penetrate the zona pellucida, usually one can fertilize the egg. After the first sperm enters, the egg releases substances that prevent other sperm from entering.

<u>As you can see, being born is a one in a million to one in ten million proportion. You are not facing those odds today.</u>

 # Notes

_____

_____

_____

_____

_____

_____

_____

_____

_____

Poverty

Poverty is one of the greatest barriers that prevent a person from traveling down the road to emancipation.

There is cruelty in poverty in that a person's mind can be engulfed with shackles of inescapability. There are institutions in place that keep individuals locked in poverty. See diagram of the institutions.

Lack of education and ignorance are also two elements of poverty. There are sincere efforts to eradicate poverty, however, most institutions do more to maintain poverty.

Benefactors from poverty are shown in the following diagram.

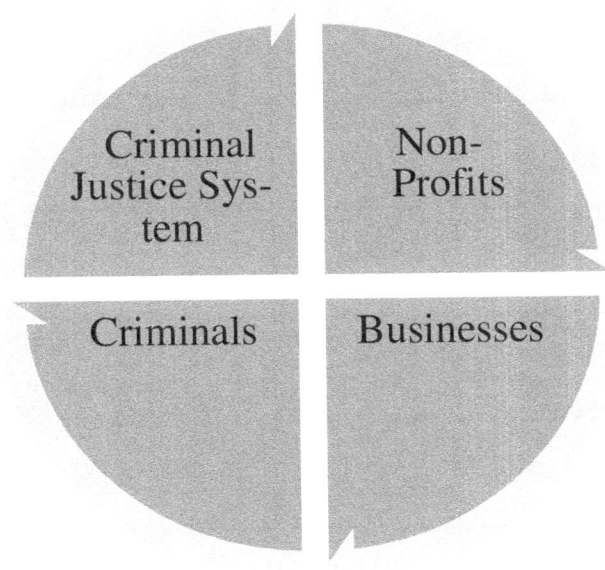

Poverty breeds many of our societal ills. What makes poverty particularly devastating is that it can be generational, and the effects of poverty are enormous. The physical and psychological toll is devastating to those caught in the cycle and to society itself.

To overcome poverty, it takes the necessary knowledge to escape its grip.

 # Notes

_____

_____

_____

_____

_____

_____

_____

_____

_____

Steps for Overcoming Poverty

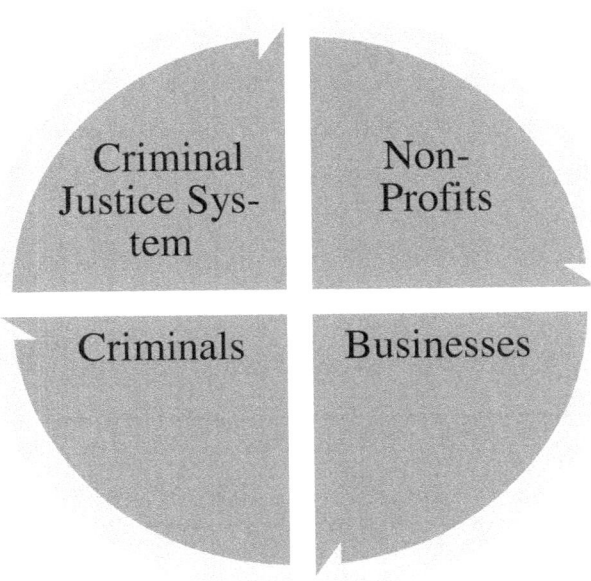

1. Education or acquiring a marketable skill
2. Expand your associations
3. Seeking knowledge
4. Overcoming the fear of change
5. Overcoming inaction and inertia
6. Setting realistic goals
7. Understanding money management

►Important Tip◄

Addiction to materialism can be just as devastating as a drug or alcohol. People who are constantly trying to keep up with the Joneses will neither be happy nor economically stable.

 # Notes

_____

_____

_____

_____

_____

_____

_____

_____

_____

6 YOUR PERSONAL GAME PLAN

Your Personal Game Plan for the Journey on the Road to Emancipation

Step 5:

- The Power of Faith
- Secure Your Physical Needs
- Healthy Triangle Assessment
- Important Tips to Embrace
- Skills for Survival
- Keys for Personal Growth
- Tips for your march towards emancipation
- Final Summary

 # Notes

_____

_____

_____

_____

_____

_____

_____

_____

_____

The Power of Faith

I intentionally end this book talking about faith. There are over seven billion people in the world. Here are some statistics to consider:

- 2.1 billion are Christians (31% of the world population), of which 50% are Catholic, 31% are Protestant, 12% Orthodox, and 1% other.
- 1.5 billion are Muslims (23% of world population) of which 87-90% are Sunnis and 10-13% Shia.
- 1.1 billion are of no religious affiliation (17%) atheist, agnostic and people who do not identify with any particular religion. One in five people (20%) in the United States are religiously unaffiliated.
- 1 billion are Hindus or (15%), the overwhelming majority (94%) of which live in India.
- 487,540,000 Buddhist (7%), half of which live in China.
- 405,120,000 Folk Religionists (6%) faiths that are closely associated with a particular group of people, ethnicity, or tribe.
- 58,110,000 other religions (1%) Baha'i, Faith Taoism, Jainism, Shintoism, Sikhism, Tenrikyo, Wicca, Zoroastrianism, and many others.
- 13 million Jews (0.2%) four-fifths of which live in two countries—United States (41%) and Israel (41%)

America is probably the most religiously diverse country in the world. I want the participants of this program to take the lessons from the five-step plan and incorporate them with their faith.

I urge participants to pursue the knowledge of their chosen faith with the same enthusiasm that you pursue your greatest passion. Faith in something more powerful than anything earthly is the key to staying on the road to emancipation. Let the knowledge of your faith be your guide to your destination and your key to locked doors.

(Source: The Pew Forum)

 # Notes

_____

_____

_____

_____

_____

_____

_____

_____

_____

_____

The Physical Needs Triangle
Secure Your Physical Needs

MIND

BODY   SOUL

1. Secure your identification card and birth certificate.
2. Educate your mind.
3. Stay active.
4. Work to improve yourself daily.
5. Begin to seek employment opportunities.
6. Be persistent.
7. Overcome your fear of failure.
8. Surround yourself with positivity.
9. Be punctual.
10. Save your money!!!

Tip: Be reasonable and practical. Make the best out of what you have. Be a bargain hunter.

 # Notes

_____

_____

_____

_____

_____

_____

_____

_____

_____

_____

Healthy Triangle Assessment

The Self Triangle

1. Have you had a physical?

2. How is your mind? Is it at peace?

3. Is your soul free from torment? Have you sought forgiveness for those you have harmed?

 # Notes

_____

_____

_____

_____

_____

_____

_____

_____

_____

_____

Important Tips to Embrace

- Become the change you want to be by absorbing in your mind the qualities needed to become the change you seek.

- Learn something daily. It's an excellent way to exercise your brain and acquire knowledge.

- Practice thinking to anticipate and react to the situations that occur in your life. Example: How do you deal with volatile situations in an environment that's unavoidable?

- Dream big—but set realistic goals and reward yourself when you achieve your goal.

- Prioritize your goals.

- Be active! Get involved in something you are passionate about.

- Never fear failure!!! The fear of failure will paralyze you from pursuing goals. Everyone fails at some point in their life.

 # Notes

_____

_____

_____

_____

_____

_____

_____

_____

_____

_____

Knowledge is Power!

Skills for Survival

- Communication Skills
- Personality Skills
- Personal Appearance/Hygiene
- Common Sense
- Education/Knowledge

 Notes

_____

_____

_____

_____

_____

_____

_____

_____

_____

_____

Keys for Personal Growth

- Knowledge of Self—who you are and your history and the history of your family.
- Knowledge of Human Nature— understanding the nature of the human species – our needs and desires.
- Knowledge of the World—understanding its people, history, and customs.
- Knowledge of the Government— understanding how our government works and affects our everyday lives.

Tips for Your March towards Emancipation

The road to emancipation is not an easy journey, so I have composed a list of things to take into consideration.

Persistence without Annoyance: remember that the people in social services, education, or any other form of services provided to the people are often overloaded. You can't assume that one phone call is all that is needed. There is a fine balancing act, however.   Remember that people who are assisting you are human beings, with problems they are personally dealing with.

Follow-up: When you are filling out applications for housing or employment, remember to follow up with phone calls or visits if necessary.

The Success in Failure: This is a contradiction, right? Not necessarily – there are times when one door is closed, and you are shown an open door without any effort. Remember that fear of failure opens no doors nor creates any opportunities.

Save Money: Remember, change saved is money earned. Don't be so quick to spend money. Some people can't stand to have money in their pocket.

Don't Obsess Over Things: Some people are not happy unless they have things. Things are replaceable. Don't be a slave to material possessions. I realize we can receive enjoyment from our material possessions, but they aren't key to our survival. Those things can be replaced.

 # Notes

_____

_____

_____

_____

_____

_____

_____

_____

_____

_____

Seek Positivity: Surround yourself with positivity. Go to community events. Give back to the community. It doesn't have to be money; it can be giving of yourself.

Take Advantage of Opportunities: Opportunity can come from doing something for others.

Final Summary: Now that we have concluded reading the five-step plan on the road to emancipation. You should have an understanding of who you are and why you are in your current condition, then design a game plan for emancipation.

Your goal is to design a plan custom fit for you in order to establish a healthy triangle. Use this book as a guide.

Sample

Goals

1. Steps toward accomplishing those goals

    Timetable (Realistic)

2. My personal plan for improvement

3. Needs to complete my goals and self-improvement plan

4. Plans for overcoming weaknesses and triggers that derail my destination

5. Atonement and reconciliation plans of action

6. Plans for expanding my knowledge

7. Plans for securing my Healthy Triangle

8. Plans for securing and maintaining my basic human needs

Buy a diary or a planner that allows you to write notes. Remember, the journey in the Game of Life is never easy, nor was it meant to be. The most important thing is to always make the wisest move possible.

 # Notes

_____

_____

_____

_____

_____

_____

_____

_____

_____

_____